OPENING DO TRADITION

The Song and Dance of Ladies Sangeet

By

Reena Kaur

CONTENTS

FOREWORD

Well done Reena for representing the ladies in our culture. I am sure your book will be a great inspiration for all women. As we from Giddha Sansaar would say "a memory and respect for our mothers, a pathway for our sisters and future for our daughters"

Jagdish

INTRODUCTION

For me the act of Singing and playing the Dholki (drum), has allowed me to connect with others. This is what a performance is about. It is dynamic and it is exciting. That excitement has fuelled my enthusiasm for this amazing art form. An art form that is in real danger of being lost to the past. In writing this book I want to put in print not just my story but the story of a proud tradition shared by many; whose roots lie in the distant past of India's history and culture. My intention is not to bore you with an in depth history of a country and its struggles but show you briefly the landscape of Music and Metaphor as well as sharing many of the songs that make the Sangeet an enduring art form.

SURVEYING THE SCENE

CHAPTER ONE

REENA KAUR – A BIOGRAPHY

Although many people think of me of having my roots in the Midlands I was actual born a Scot. Born in the most beautiful and most artistic of all Scottish cities, Edinburgh. Windblown and hewn from the volcanic rock of the past it is a beautiful City and one I intend visiting again soon.

It was not to last long though and at the age of 12 months I was moved to the North of England and then onto Telford. A far cry cry from the Highlands of Scotland. I sometimes wonder what my voice would have sounded like with an Edinburgh accent! I did indeed return to Scotland when I was 8 years old, taking part in a pageant at the Edinburgh Festival.

My mother was actually born in Liverpool so you might here a northern twang now and again...

I left Telford 19 years later to marry a man in Birmingham and have lived here ever since and from that moment on my life was to change.

How was I to know that I was standing on the threshold of change!

I had always sang and enjoyed singing from any early age but my career did not really start until I was 25. Prior to that

I was involved in Beauty and Cosmetics working for a large cosmetics company.

I think it was here that I realised I had an affinity to get on with people. To be able to build rapport naturally and I enjoyed that time.

I had always had a dream that I was going to be successful, but with an arranged marriage pending those dreams would be put on hold. I felt that as a single Indian girl of 18 my dreams would be put on hold for a while. I had many ambitions and goals that would be difficult, if not impossible to fulfil.

I left school with no formal qualifications but had a passion and desire to work in beauty and fashion.

Once I had left school I started teaching dance whilst pursuing my own study of beauty. It was at this time I found Mary Kay Cosmetics. They pushed me and made many of my dreams come true. Their support and their belief in me drove me on. They were my saviours at that time.

It was then that I realised I could work for myself and became a freelance Make-up artist. It gave me liberation of a sort and I was successful in this venture to the point of building a large customer base and started working for magazines. I worked for some major fashion department stores whilst working as a beautician privately. I even reached the point where I produced my own branding and was getting a name for myself. I was also the leading make up artist/stylist where I was responsible for a wide range of the top models on that show.

It was during this time that my marriage was starting to fall apart. It was a tough time. In retrospect however it turned out to be an important time in my life and it made me the woman I am today. Stronger, and more independent with a sense of resolve. I knew I could do anything and I didn't need a man to help.

It was strange because, as soon as I had made this decision a door had opened on the world and I was gaining true freedom.

As a woman, and up until this point, I felt that I couldn't get on with- out the help of a man...how wrong I was! My youngest child was Five when my husband left us. I had to work and I didn't want to depend on the state for a living. In order to supplement my self-employment I also worked in Promotions just to keep food on the table and a roof over my children's' heads. During this period I had many difficulties both personally and in my job and by coincidence fell into my role as a singer. The journey was about to start!

Jagdish made it all happen for me. I knew Jag from when I had my second child and he had always been a great supporter. He's a well known dancer from Nachda Sansaar a group of Punjabi Folk Dancers from Birmingham. I'd always been a big fan. I'd always been into the folk songs and after that conversation we always kept in touch.

I remember as a child being captivated by the old Punjabi Folk Songs and in particular by the Dholki. I was inspired from an early age by my Aunt who used to play at family parties and I recall sitting there watching and being excited by the sounds coming out of this drum. It was an important time for me and would impact my life forever.

One day...out of the blue, I think it was early 2000 Jag got in touch to tell me someone was looking for a singer. I was shocked and said I wasn't able to.

I felt that I wasn't good enough and doubts clouded my mind. I just couldn't see the potential that Jag obviously saw a fter thinking it through and agonising about whether I was good enough or not, I thought I would just do it and see what would happen.

The booking was made and I agreed to do it only to find out that it had been cancelled and the work had fallen through! This was maybe 6 years ago... then suddenly despite this shaky start I started to gain a reputation and once one door had opened more followed soon thereafter. I was gaining recognition.

Many friends advised me and said that I had a great voice that would only get better if I took singing lessons. It was through these lessons that I met some of the greatest singing teachers and of course their network of contacts. They give me so much encouragement that I never wanted to stop. During this time I even released a single which was played on Raaj FM. It was a duet with the well known singer Manny Khaira. Unknown to me he was a great supporter of my work.

The song and I got so much publicity it was amazing. Bearing in mind I was still, at this point involved in my Cosmetics business. It was a very tiring but rewarding time.

This was to be a turning point for me as I was soon taken to do a show in Italy with Manny. I couldn't believe it! we were a massive hit out there and I was on a high. Things were happening now and I was being taken seriously. My confidence and self belief were at an all time high and I felt vindicated. The sacrifices were worth it and doors were beginning to open for me.

We flew back from Italy to do another show in Birmingham which was another success. Manny and I then decided that things were going so well we should sing together and produce the song as a free download. We had 70,000 hits immediately on Youtube, and this was a traditional Punjabi folksong!

It was an old song that we gave new life too.

It was because of this that I was getting even more exposure and the Ladies Sangeet concept grew.

Ladies Sangeet had been dying out in the UK. There was, it seemed no one performing these songs and I felt it was time for a rebirth of this genre. It seemed sad to me that such an ancient tradition was being left behind and would soon be lost to future generations. I felt it was my responsibility to rekindle the flame. To keep that tradition alive for a new audience before it was too late.

I found that I would often surprise some of the older listeners who had, perhaps forgotten the songs, and they would be surprised that here was a young woman, British born, singing the old songs once again. Giving life to them. So much joy will be lost if this tradition vanishes. The sad thing is it will unless we promote it wholeheartedly.

To me Ladies Sangeet is a chance for women to get together and celebrate. Traditionally this would be at a wedding but it is often done when women get together to celebrate any life event. There's always a song for every event! They are blessings too and for example they say that at the beginning of an event you perform 5 blessing songs and they are sang by women only at these events. There are specific songs for boys just as there are for girls. Details of these will appear later in the book. The songs all have their own narrative. They are songs with a meaning and songs with a purpose.

As well as using my voice I am also a very capable Dholki player. The Dholki is a traditional double ended drum and I use it as the accompaniment to the songs.

It is an instrument that is more often than not played exclusively in the Ladies Sangeet. I often get asked to play the dholki at various musical functions and often alongside other musicians but I decline.

The Ladies Sangeet is all about the voice with its stories and the drum that beats out a specific rhythm that gives energy to the song.

I am also aware that when I perform the Sangeet women are brought together in a fundamental way. I am a sikh and I'm aware that within Indian culture there exists the caste system This is an ancient system that can only divide people , keeping them apart. I believe that as an English born Sikh the caste system should not prevent us women getting together and actually I've found that the Sangeet brings us closer. There should be no place for the caste system in the Sangeet. Indeed I have performed the Sangeet for Hindus and Muslims and I feel very strongly that we are all just people with differing beliefs who should be able to share this rich cultural tradition.

I don't see the Sangeet as a religious thing any way. At least not something that is exclusively Sikh or Muslim or Hindu. Its a celebration for life and life should encompass all!

The primary instrument, and this is definitely the only one I use, is the Dholkhi. This is a large drum and I can play this to accompany my singing. It's about as keeping it as simple as possible. My voice and the back beat of the drum.

Whilst I have had many comments on the purity of my voice I find that its just as important to be a people person. What I mean by that is that I love being around people and love what I do. This comes across, I think when I'm singing and when I meet people. It's that connection I find important and I feel I have a natural empathy with others. It's not enough to be able to sing...I love performing and I love to get others involved. I often get others to sing with me and we take turns to sing a verse each or maybe the chorus. Sometimes we all sing and I simply lead the proceedings. It has and should have a sense of community. A bringing together and a binding together of a community of women. I encourage them to get up and dance along with the song and the rhythm. It's a participant sport not a spectator sport.

In the past the Sangeet was for women only but now men get involved although they are not encouraged to sing! They tend to dance.

At first sight it may seem that I only talk about the Sangeet in terms of women but I had a major influence in my life and he was male. My Grandfather was a Dholki Master and he taught me to play. Both sides of the family had children. Lots of them! So when we had family get togethers it was a huge party and we would dance and sing to the sound of the Drum. It was so exciting and I was so young and memories flood back whenever I hear the Dholki. It was a huge influence on my life.

I guess I got the musical skills from my grandfather and I guess its in the genes. He was along with my Aunty such a great influence.

In India there were few professional musicians and it was very difficult if you weren't wealthy. It was a real struggle for him and he wouldn't have made any money. He would have had to work to sustain his family and play the dholki for the entertainment of others.

This then, is the tradition I feel I am continuing. Now that the doors have been opened I need to let others see what I see and feel what I feel when taking part in the ladies Sangeet.

I continue to sing and continue to learn about The Sangeet and run workshops and tuition for both the voice and the

drum. With the rise and development of Social media the time has come to bring this Proud tradition in to the 21st century via this medium of communication.

CHAPTER TWO

Sangeet: A Brief History of Indian Folk Music

Indian folk music has a richness and diversity unlike any other because of vast cultural heritage and tradition. It's development grew, it is believed, through the early religious devotional songs extant at that time in Asia. As time went on these songs would be inclusive of every aspect of the human condition. In many of these songs we see insight into existence itself. The psychology, social and economic conditions of mankind as well as philosophy and all that entails was being included.

Despite these changes they were, and still are, considered to be of profound religious importance serving to aid a persons development through song and dance.

There were many important and eminent bards/ saints or Fakirs who contributed to this field. Names like Kabi

Moinuddin Chishti, Lalon Fakir and more. You can get more information on these from sources I have mentioned in the bibliography.

The songs were naturally classified by their regional languages. Linguistics obviously affect the structure and their emphasis and at the present time songs come in many forms including Bhangra,

lavani, dandiya and Rajasthani. These actually were the ones with the strongest connections to the past.

With The arrival of technology and particularly movies and pop music, folk music waned in popularity and was in real danger of being lost to the past, hence my desire to bring them back into use but this time in the modern western world.

I think it's important for the reader to understand how deeply embedded the Folk tradition is in India's culture and therefore I have included a list of the various styles and techniques with a brief description giving the reader an idea of how widespread this tradition really is.

- 1. Bhavageete
- 2 Bhangra and Giddha

- 3 Bihugeet

- 4 Lavani

- 5 Uttarakhandi Music

- 6. Dandiya

- 7 Pandavani

- 8 Bauls

- 9 Bhatiali

- 10 Garba

- 11 Dollu Kunita

- 12 Kolata/Kolattam

- 13 Veeragase

Below I have listed the areas of India where the various forms are still practiced. It is by no means an exhaustive list and is here to bring you up to date with what is happening in India.

- Gujarat: Garba,Doha

- Andhra Pradesh: Madiga Dappu, Mala Jamidika

- Assam: Bihugeet, Tokarigeet, Kamrupi Lokgeet,

Goalparia Lokogeet

- Chhattisgarh: Pandavani

- Karnataka: Bhavageete, Dollu Kunita, Veeragase

- Maharashtra: Lavani

- Punjab: Bhangra

- Tamil Nadu: Naatupura Paatu

- West Bengal: Baul, Bhatiali, Bhadu, Bhawayia, Saari, LokGeeti, PalliGeeti

- Kerala: Pulaya, Paraya,

Bhavageete

Bhavageete (literally 'emotion poetry') is a form of expressionist poetry often accompanied by light music. Most of the poetry sung in this genre pertain to subjects like love, nature, philosophy, etc., and the genre itself is not much different from Ghazals, though Ghazals are bound to a peculiar metre. This genre is quite popular in many parts of India, notably in Karnataka. Bhavageete may be called by different names in other languages.

Kannada Bhavageete draws from the poetry of modern, including Kuvempu, D. R. Bendre, Gopalakrishna Adiga, K.S. Narasimhaswamy, G.S. Shivarudrappa, K. S. Nissar Ahmed , N S Lakshminarayana Bhatta etc. Notable Bhavageete performers include P. Kalinga Rao, Mysore

Ananthaswamy, C. Aswath, Shimoga Subbanna, Archana Udupa, Raja Ananthaswamy etc.

Bhangra And Giddha

Bhangra: is a form of dance -oriented folk-music of Punjab.. The present musical style is derived from non traditional musical accompaniment to the riffs of Punjab called by the same name. The female dance of Punjab region Giddhais known as Giddha.

The roots of Bhangra music date back to the early 1980s, when several Punjabi bands started experimenting with Western styles as well as traditional Punjabi music. Significant amongst these were 'The Black Mist', 'The Shots', 'The Jambo Boys', 'Heera' and 'The Saathies'. However, the first recording artist/group of this type of music in the UK was Bhujangy Group, founded by brothers

Balbir Singh Khanpur and Dalbir Singh Khanpur in Birmingham in 1967. Bhujhangy Group's first major hit was "Bhabiye Akh Larr Gayee" in the early 1970s, released on Birmingham's Oriental Star Agencies label. This was the first song to combine traditional Asian music with modern western instruments, which would be followed by further developments of this in bhangra.

Bhangra music was founded in London by P u n j a b i immigrants who took their native folk music and began experimenting by altering it using instruments from their host country. Bhangra music is one of the few immigrant music genres of the world that is absent in the home country.

The new genre quickly became popular in Britain replacing Punjabi folk singers due to it being heavily influenced in Britain by the infusion of rock music and a need to move away from the simple and repetitive Punjabi folk music. It indicated the development of a self-conscious and distinctively rebellious British Asian youth culture centred on an experiential sense of self, e.g., language, gesture, bodily signification, desires, etc., in a situation in which tensions with British culture and racist elements in British society had resulted in alienation in many minority ethnic groups, fostered a sense of need for an affirmation of a positive identity and culture, and provided a platform for British Punjabi males to assert their masculinity.

Bihugeet

Bihugeet is a traditional folk music of Assam, performed through Bihu dance in the festival of Bihu. The songs have themes of romance, love, nature and real life situations. The dance is celebrated in groups with young girls and boys being the main participants.

Lavani

Lavani is a popular folk form of Maharashtra . Traditionally, the songs are sung by female artists,

but male artists may occasionally sing Lavanis The dance format associated with Lavani is known as Tamasha. This dance format contains the dancer (Tamasha Bai), the helping dancer - Maavshi, The Drummer - Dholki vaala & The Flute Boy - Baasuri Vaala.

Uttarakhandi music

Uttarakhandi folk music had its roots in the lap of nature. The pure and blessed music have the feel and the touch of nature and subjects related to nature. The folk music primarily is related to the festivals, religious traditions, folk stories and simple life of the people of Uttarakhand. Thus the songs of Uttarakhand are a true reflection of the cultural heritage and the way people live their lives in the Himalayas. Musical instruments used in Uttarakhand music include the dhol, damoun, turri, ransingha, dholki, daur, thali, bhankora and masakbhaja. Tabla and harmonium are also used but to a lesser extent. The main languages are Kumaoni and Garhwali

Dandiya

Dandiya is a dance-oriented folk music that has also been adapted for pop music worldwide, popular in Western India, especially during Navaratri. The present musical style is derived from the traditional musical accompaniment to the folk dance of Dandiya called by the same name.

Pandavani

Pandavani is a folk singing style of musical narration of tales from ancient epic Mahabharata with musical accompaniment and Bhima as hero. This form of folk theatre is popular in the state of Chhattisgarh and in the neighbouring tribal areas of Orissa and Andhra Pradesh.

Rajasthani music has a diverse collection of musician castes, including langas, sapera, bhopa, jogi and Mangania.

Bauls

The Bauls of Bengal were an order of musicians in 18th, 19th and early 20th century India who played a form of music using a Khama, ektara and dotara. The word Baul comes from Sanskritbatul meaning divinely inspired insanity. They are a group of Hindu mystic minstrels.

They are thought to have been influenced greatly by the Hindu tantric sect of the Kartabhajas as well as by Sufi sects. Bauls travel in search of the internal ideal, Maner Manush (Man of the Heart).

Bhatiali

This type of music was cultured mainly by the oarsmen & fishermen of Bengal. There are many opinions regarding the origin of the term Bhatiali. Most popular of them are:

- They use to sing it in the Ebb (Bhata) as in this phase it does not need much effort for rowing

- It originated from the Bhati area (now in Bangladesh).

One of the most eminent singers is Nirmalendu Chowdhur

Garba

Garba ("song") is sung in honor of Hindu goddesses god during Navratri. They are sung in the honor of god Krishna,Hanuman, Ram, etc.

Dollu Kunita

This is a group dance that is named after the Dollu — the percussion instrument used in the dance. It is performed by the menfolk of the Kuruba community of the North Karnataka area. The group consists of 16 dancers who wear the drum and beat it to rhythms while dancing. The beat is controlled and directed by a leader with cymbals who is positioned in the centre. Slow and fast rhythms alternate and group weaves varied patterns.

Kolata/Kolattam

Kolata/Kolattam is a traditional folk dance of the states of Andhra Pradesh, Karnataka and Tamil Nadu. Similar to its North Indian counterpart Dandiya Ras, it is performed with coloured sticks and usually involves both men and women dancing together.

Veeragase

Veeragase is a dance folk form prevalent in the state of Karnataka. It is a vigorous dance based on Hindu mythology and involves very intense energy- sapping dance movements. Veeragase is one of the dances demonstrated in the Dasara procession held in Mysore.

Sangeet: A Brief History of Sangeet in Asian Culture

The term Sangeet is from Sanskrit which when translated into English simply means: Sung Together...

The Sangeet ceremony traditionally usually will take place 5, 7 or 9 days before a wedding and is a Punjabi (Indian/

Pakistani) ceremony. In ages past the sangeet was the reserve of women only but some sangeet have both men and women involved. It is a time for celebration, singing, dancing, joking and having a good time. Traditional Indian instruments are often used and in particular the Dholki (two sided drum).

Historically Sangeet is a threefold art- form of vocal music, instrumental music and dance. Since classical dance is also a component, it is not strictly synonymous with the western term "music". There is of course a historical reason for this and in the Vedic and post Vedic period it was customary to perform mythical dramas. These dramas used dancers to mime the story, instrumentalists to play the music and vocalists to tell the stories. Dance is referred to as "nritya", vocal is referred to as "gayaki" and instrumental is known as "vadhya sangeet"

This vocal tradition is especially strong in Indian music. It is probably true to say that singing is the earliest form of music. One may also argue that the Samaveda is the oldest musical text in India. However it is probably more pertinent to look at contemporary music to define what we mean by Sangeet in the modern world. Musical forms are made up and built on very well defined structures. These structures such as primary theme, secondary theme and other elements form a stretchered framework in which improvisation plays a key role.

There are many genres both old and new.

Dhrupad and dhammar are some of the oldest in use today and they go as far back as the Mogul empires (16th century) Equally old but stylistically different is the tarana which is based upon meaningless syllables. More modern are the highly improvised kheyal, dadra and thumri. In the Punjab there is also the tappa.

Most of the classical songs of north India are devotional in nature but there a still a few orientated toward religiosity.

For the hindus: bhajan, dhun or kirtan For Muslims: kawali

And the Sikhs: Shabad

For the not so serious there are many popular genres. The gazal is rich in its poetic and romantic style. The hindi geet is just a song.

We must not forgot too the educational use of this genre. The most notable is of course the lakshan geet In this style the words of the song actually describe the rag which is being performed.

We must look at mythology to really see the significance that Indian music(sangeet) has to Indian society. This is easily illustrated in the story concerning its origin. Perhaps the clearest mythological raison-detre may be found in Bharata's Natya-Shastra

Once, a long time ago, during the transitional period between two Ages it so happened that people took to uncivilised ways, were ruled by lust and greed, behaved in angry and jealous ways with each other and not only gods but demons, evil spirits, yakshas and and such like others swarmed over the earth. Seeing this plight, Indra and other gods approached god Brahma and requested him to give the people a toy (Kridaniyaka), but one which could not only be seen but heard and this should turn out a diversion (so that people gave up their bad ways)

Although it was decided to give the celestial art of sangeet to mankind, a suitable human had to be found who was capable of receiving this gift. Sangeet had always been in the realm of the demigods (gandharva. A super-human of superior spiritual ability was required to convey this celestial art-form to the world of man. It fell upon the great sage Narada to be the first mortal recipient of this divine art. Through Narada, we are indebted for the presence of classical music.

The introduction of this art-form to the mortal world was only the first step. Traditional pedagogy had to accommodate it. Classical music is considered more than mere entertainment; it is a moral and spiritual redeemer. Therefore, the divine qualities inherent in the art-form imply certain prerequisites; key among them are guru, vinaya and sadhana. This translates to teacher, humility, and discipline. The guru, or teacher is the most important prerequisite in traditional musical pedagogy. Music is said to be a guru mukha-vidhya

(i.e., knowledge which must come from a teacher). This is considered the highest form of knowledge. Traditional pedagogy is based upon the transfer of knowledge from the teacher (guru) to the disciple (shishya in an unbroken tradition (parampara). The tradition of guru-shishya-parampara extends back countless millennia. The second prerequisite is vinaya (humility). This also reflects the divine origins of the art-form. Classical music is said to be a worship that involves both the listener and the artist alike. Any negative emotions such as arrogance (abhiman) becomes an impediment. This is an impediment from both the divine aspect as well as a matter of simple pedagogy (e.g., "If you think you already know everything, then what is there to learn?") The final prerequisite for a student of classical music is sadhana (discipline and practice). Sadhana is necessary at two levels. At one level, the divine origins of the art-form require that the student "be prepared" to be a recipient of this knowledge. However, from a simple pedagogic standpoint, the music is so incredibly difficult that if the student does not devote countless hours of practice spread over many years, the student certainly will not be able to master the music.

This may clarify many points of pedagogy, but what about the art-form itself? Any art must deal with the topic of aesthetics. The Indian tradition has much to say on this point as well.

The ancient scriptures describe nine fundamental emotions from which all complex emotions may be produced. Just as all hues may be produced by mixing the three primary colours, so too, all emotions are said to be derived from these principal emotions . They are called navaras and are shown in the table below. These emotions form the aesthetic foundation for sangeet. We must remember that we are talking about music. This requires an acoustic vehicle to convey these emotions.

The Nine Moods (Nava Rasa) Shringar - Love

Hasya - Comic Karuna - Sadness Raudra - Furious Veera - Heroic Bhayanak - Terrible

Vibhats - Disgusting

Adbhuta - Wonderment Shanta - Peace

This acoustic vehicle is known as rag. Rag may be thought of as the melodic foundation upon which classical Indian music is based. During the last few centuries it was customary to anthropomorphize the rag in the form of gandharvas (demigods) and apsaras (celestial nymphs).

The divine quality of music is perhaps best illustrated in nad siddha. This is the ability to perform miracles by singing or playing certain rags. The most famous miracle-working musician was Tansen. It is often said that he was able to create fire by singing rag Dipak, or create rain by singing rag Megh Malhar.

We have seen how this art-form is considered divine. This divine quality influences concepts such as aesthetics and pedagogy. The reverence that Indians have for this system may only be seen in a traditional approach.

However this does not bar us from taking a more objective approach.

STANDING ON THE THRESHOLD

CHAPTER THREE

The Wedding Tradition
Instruments and Song

THE WEDDING TRADITION

The following outline is not exhaustive and is meant to convey the main ideas that surround the Ladies Sangeet. These ceremonies are performed 9, 7 and/ or 5 days before the actual wedding takes place

ROKA:

This is the first step where meeting of two family members is arranged at brides home and the grooms immediate family members are invited. The word Roka means 'to stop'And in this perspective it is to stop the search of partner as the perfect match has been found

TAKA:

The word Taka means to 'set the date' After roka this ceremony is conceded at brides place to set wedding date and preparations are made for engagement

KURMAI(Engagement):

This is a formal engagement ceremony which is performed at grooms place or gurdhwara.

Family members are invited and groom presents the engagement ring. This is also when the brides family members offer kara (sikh steel bangle) to the groom. Engagement ceremony is started with a short prayer by granthi (sikh priest). After which red scarf is placed around the grooms shoulder along

with dried dates according to granthis instruction and then grandfather feeds that dried dated to the groom after which food and drinks are enjoyed by all.

CHUNNI CEREMONY:

This ceremony is performed by mother of the groom who cover the brides head with chuuni (red scarf) which represents that from now onwards she is responsible for upholding the honour and pride of her family. Bride is dressed in clothing and jewelery by her inlaws. Groom marks her head with sindoor (red powder) as sign of commitment.

Grooms parents offer shagun (sweets) to bride and her family as blessings and acceptance of engagement. Gifts are exchanged followed by lavish celebration with lot of music and dance take place.

MAIYA(cleansing and purifying):

This function is performed by both families at their respective homes. This ceremony should be perform for 5days in total before wedding. Oil is brushed into bride and grooms hair with olive branches, and their body is massaged with turmeric powder. Girls performing maiya has red string (thread) tied around their wrist, during this ceremony red scraf is hold above the bride or groom's head. At each corner of the scarf girls take turn to hold scarf and traditional songs are sung and enjoyed by all.

KARAHI CHARNA:

This ceremony is performed 5 days before the wedding till the d-day at the bride and grooms respective home. Savory and sweet items are cooked in large dish (karahi). Guest visiting home are served with appetizer as a gesture of blessing to bride and groom.

NANKI SHAK:

In this process gifts are exchanged at bride and grooms respective home leading by the uncle. Sometimes a priest performs small pooja (ceremony) before exchange of gift or this ceremony can be formal get together.

MEHENDI:

This ceremony is performed 1or 2 days before wedding. Bride and groom both are adorned with henna (mehendi), the hand and feet are adorned with mehendi (henna), eucalyptus oil, clove oil and lemon juice water. Traditional dholak or Dholki is played and the women enjoy themselves with folk dance and song. This when the Sangeet is performed. Ladies in the house also apply mehendi on their hands and leg as it is known as shagun. Mehendi is suppose to be symbolize the love of couple, darker the colour, stronger is the love.

CHOORA ceremony (bangel ceremony):

This ceremony is performed at brides maternal home by her uncle giving her choora (21 bangel with red and cream color) which is bathed in lassi (yoghurt milk) and rosewater. Traditional folk songs are enjoyed by all the guest. After putting the choora the uncle covers it with shawl (subar) which represents breaking away from natural family and home. Kaliras (silver and gold hanging ornaments) are tied on the bangels by everyone blessing bride. Before leaving the room she touches one of her female friends with kalirah and its been said whosever head it falls next would be her wedding.

INSTRUMENTS AND SONG

The Dholki

The Dholki is a South Asian two-headed hand-drum and is related to the Punjabi Dhol and the larger Dholak.

It may have traditional cotton rope lacing, screw- turnbuckle tensioning or both combined: in the first case steel rings are used for tuning or pegs are twisted inside the laces.

The dholak is mainly

a folk instrument, lacking the exact tuning and playing techniques of the tabla or the pakhawaj. The drum is pitched, depending on size, with an interval of perhaps a perfect fourth or perfect fifth between the two heads.

Construction

The smaller surface of the dholki is made of goat skin for sharp notes and the bigger surface is made of buffalo skin for low pitches, which allows a combination of bass and treble with rhythmic high and low pitches

The shell is sometimes made from sheesham wood but cheaper dholaks may be made from any wood, such as mango. Sri Lankan dholaks and dholkis are made from hollowedcoconut palm stems.

Usage

It is widely usedin quawalli, kirtan, lavani and bhangra. It was formerly used in classical dance and as previously stated with religious connotations. Indian children sing and dance to it during pre- wedding festivities. It is often used in Filmi Sangeet (Indian film music), in chutney music, baithak gana, tan singing, and the local Indian music of Jamaica, Suriname, Guyana and Trinidad and Tobago, where it was brought by indentured immigrants. In the Fiji Islands the dholak is widely used for bhajan and

kirtan. It is mostly used in India. The dholak's higher-pitched head is a simple membrane while the bass head, played usually with the left hand, has a compound syahi to lower the pitch and enable the typical Dholak sliding sound (" giss" or "gissa"), often the caked residue of mustard oil pressing, to which some sand and oil or tar may be added. The Sri Lankan uses a large fixed tabla-style syahi on the middle of the bass skin.

In Pakistan, it is used during weddings by family members to sing folk and wedding songs at events known as dholkis. This is the type of drum I play.

Playing style

The drum is either played on the player's lap or, while standing, slung from the shoulder or waist or pressed down with one knee while sitting on the floor.

In some styles of playing (such as Punjab) an iron thumb ring is used to produced a distinctive "chak" rim sound. In other styles (such as Rajasthani), all fingers are generally used.

Dholak masters are often adept at singing or chanting and may provide a primary entertainment or lead drumming for a dance troupe. Perhaps the most characteristic rhythm played on the dhol is a quick double-dotted figure that may be counted in rhythmic solfege as "ONE -tah and -tah TWO -tah and -tah THREE-E -TAH, FOUR AND" (rest on "and") or simply a long string of double-dotted notes, over which the bass side is used for improvisation.

On large dholaks, known as dhols, the high-pitched head may be played using a thin (1/4" / 6 mm or less) long (over 14" / 30 cm) stick of rattan or bamboo (rattan is preferred for its flexibility) and the low-pitched drum head using a somewhat thicker, angled stick.

Variants

The dholki (Hindi/Urdu: pipe or tube) is often a bit narrower in diameter and uses tabla-style syahi masala on its treble skin. This instrument is also known as the naal. Its treble skin is stitched onto an iron ring, similarly to East Asian Janggu or Shime- daiko drums, which tenses the head before it is fitted. The bass skin often has the same structure as in ordinary dholak, being fitted on to a bamboo ring, but sometimes they have a kinar and pleated

Gajra, as seen in tabla to withstand the extra tension. Sri Lankan dholkis have high quality skins with syahi on both sides, producing a sound like a very high-pitched tabla and using a simplified tabla fingering. Steel tuning rings are not used - instead, wooden pegs are twisted to create a very high tension. The heads are created with triple stitching to withstand tension. Similar dholkis are in use in Maharashtra and elsewhere. Heavy hardwood dholaks are said[to produce better sound than those carved of cheap unseasoned sapwood Similar drums with similar names are found elsewhere in western Asia.

CHAPTER FOUR

Crossing Cultures

Music,, like the other arts is what feeds the soul and touches the body, moving it and energising it. Anyone who has grown up with music around them as I did, knows the tremendous effect it has on ones memory and their life. My memories are what shape me and what shape the collective unconscious. They either divide or bring together people and cultures. In such a divisive world music seems to be the common denominator that closes the divide and unites. This is why I love to sing.

Music can fit our moods as well, and is a powerful anchor that motivates and stimulates our behaviours. Sometimes we are in harmony with the song and with whatever the rhythm says to us. It nurtures, comforts, commiserated, exhilarates, soothes and strengthens us against the Unknown. What would life be without it.?

Whenever I sing and whenever I play I am conscious of the effect it has on those involved. That's what a performance is about. Always remember: the meaning of communication is the response you get...always. When I sing I sing from the heart and my spirit sings too and as I watch the audience around me I know that no matter what the culture, whatever the religion we are all singing the same song.

This for me is what the Sangeet is all about and hope that you get as much out of it as I do...

OPENING THE DOOR

CHAPTER FIVE

Songs of Ladies Sangeet

Whilst not exhaustive I have included below a number of songs from my tradition. I hope you will learn them and sing them passing them onto to the next generation in order we keep this genre alive.

Gadhi teri veera (Boys Ghori-blessing)

The Ghori Charna is the final ceremony at the groom's place. The groom's sisters and cousins feed and adorn his mare. To ward off the evil eye, people use cash and perform the Varna ritual. The cash is then distributed among the poor. In ancient times the boy would climb on a horse and leave his home for the wedding venue.

Gadhi teri veera, veh steel di bani
Chup beja veera, veh shakeen bana keh
Babul tera veera veh ajj rusiya phireh
veh manaleh veera janjh soni saajeh
Gadhi teri veera, veh steel di bani

Chup beja veera, veh shakeen bana

keh Veera tera veera ajj rusiya phireh

Veh manahleh veera janjh soni saajeh

Gadhi teri veera, veh steel di bani

Chup beja veera, veh shakeen bana keh

Daaha tera veera ajj rusiya phireh

Veh manahleh veera janjh soni saajeh

Gadhi teri veera, veh steel di bani

Chup beja veera, veh shakeen bana keh

Nanna tera veera ajj rusiya phireh

Veh manahleh veera janjh soni saajeh

Gadhi teri veera, veh steel di bani

Chup beja veera, veh shakeen bana keh

Thaya tera veera ajj rusiya phireh

Veh manahleh veera janjh soni saajeh

Gadhi teri veera, veh steel di bani

Chup beja veera, veh shakeen bana keh

Chacha tera veera ajj rusiya phireh

Veh manahleh veera janjh soni saajeh

Translation (Brother your car is made out of steel, sit in it suited and booted All the male relatives in your family are sulking, make peace with them so your wedding party will be beautiful)

Sehreh waliya Maan Jawaniya (Boys Ghori blessing)

Sehre waliya maan jawaniya

Maa pyou dah tu dil naa thori veh…

Pena wallo much na morri vehn

Nekhadiya neh eho he nishaniya

Rakhi beeba chaa he chaa veh penna dah tu maa wadaah veh

Nekhadiya neh eho he nishaniya

Sehrewaliya maan jawaaniya

Kathiya ho keh sabeh ayeeya, ral mil teriya chichi the thahiya

Kiriya jakeh veehra sahra

Phabiya da tu diyor pyara

Tereh uthe veera mein phool barsoniya

Seereh waliya maan jawaaniya

Seereh waliya maan jawaaniya

Translation (Handsome groom may you be blessed and evils keep kept away from you,don't break your parents heart and don't turn your back on your sisters as these are the signs of humbleness, through your happiness you will make your sisters very proud,

Everyone has gathered together as you are very loved and I want to shower you with flowers.)

Hirani (Geet – song)

Tu mrea sardar, veh mein teri hirani aah Shava mein teri hirani aah

Tu mera sardar veh mein teri hirani aah Shava mein teri hirani aah

Kuteh uteh aye veh Ranjha mein payah taak ni aah raah

Kuhteh uteh aye veh Ranjha mein payah taak ni aah raah

Na mukh mori na dil tori menu teri chaah!

Veh mein teri hirani aah shava mein teri hirani aah

Tu mera sardar veh mein teri hirani aah shava mein teri hirani aah

Bhaageh wich aya karo, bhaageh wich aya karo

Jaah veh jaah ranjhana mera dil naa dukhaya karo ,

jaah veh jaah ranjhna mera dil naah dukhaya karo

Katcheh karreh teh tharkeh ajja ikk warri kardu haa

katcheh karreh teh tharkeh ajja ikk warri kardu haa

Sachi tereh pyar deh uthou warra apni jaan

Veh mein teri soni aah tu mera

Mehiwaal teh mein teri Sonia aah

Shava mein teri Soni aah

Tu mrea sardar, veh mein teri hirani aah

Shava mein teri hirani aah

Tu mrea sardar, mein teri hirani aah

Shava mein teri hirani aah

Shava mein teri hirani aah

Shava mein teri hirani aah

Shava mein teri hirani aah

Translation (You are my Mr Singh my chief and I am your dear, come to the top roof my Romeo I am waiting for you, don't break my heart please don't be upset with me as I really like you, just come to me once I will be yours forever. You are my mr singh my chief and I am your dear.)

Niki Sooie watma dhaaga (Suhaag Girls blessing)

Niki sooie watma dhaaga

Beteh kasidaah kadraiya, bararu aya raajeh da beta

Tu que bibi rhonraiya

Babul mera saaha sadiya mata meri dhaaj banaya

mein pardesan horaiya

Niki sooie watma dhaaga

Beteh keh haar parohraiya, Ondeh jandeh rahi puch

deh tu que bibi rhonraiya

Veereh mereh kaaj rechayia bhabi meri dhaaj banaya mein
pardesan horaiya
Niki sooie watma dhaaga

Beteh kasidaah kadraiya, Ondeh jandeh rahi puch
deh tu que bibi rhonraiya
Thaiya mereh kaaj rechayia Thaiye meri dhaaj
banaya mein pardesan horaiya
Niki sooie watma dhaaga
Beteh keh haar parohraiya, Ondeh jandeh rahi puch deh tu
que bibi rhonraiya
Chacha mereh kaaj rechayia Chachii meri dhaaj banaya
mein pardesan horaiya
Niki sooie watma dhaaga
Beteh kasidaah kadraiya, Ondeh jandeh rahi puch deh tu
que bibi rhonraiya
mameh mereh kaaj rechayia mami meri dhaaj banaya mein
pardesan horaiya
Mein padesan horaiya Mein pardesan horaiya
Haan mein pardesan horaiya…

**Translation (Little needle and cotton thread, im sitting
sowing, from outside comes the prince and askes me why**

are you crying, I tell him my father is getting me married my mother is preparing my dowry as they are sending me far away…)

Sadah Chiriyan da chamba (Suhaag Girls blessing)

Sadah chiriyan da chamba veh babul asa udh janna Sadi lambi udaahri veh babul kereh des janna Sadah chiriyan da chamba veh babul asa udh janna Sadi lambi udaahri veh babul kereh des janna
Teriyan mehla deh wich wich veh babul mera dholla areya
Teriyan mehala deh wich wich veh babul mera dholla areya
Ikk itt puta devan, dheeyeh ghar ja apaneh
Sadah chiriyan da chamba veh babul asa udh janna Sadi lambi udaahri veh babul kereh des janna Teriyan mehala de vich vich veh babul gudiyain khon khedeh
Meriyan kedhan phothariya dheeyeh ghar jaah apaneh
Sadah chiriyan da chamba veh babul asa udh janna Sadi lambi udaahri veh babul kereh des janna
Teriya bhagha wich wich veh babul charkha kona katheh
Meriyan kathan pothariyan dheeyeh ghar jaah apaneh
Sadah chiriyan da chamba veh babul asa udh janna Sadi lambi udaahri veh babul kereh des jann

Translation (I am a bird in a cage father I am going to fly away, im awaiting my father which city will you send me to, father sings back saying you have to go to your own house now my daughter that is the place for you)

Lateh di chadar (Geet-song)

Lateh di chadar uteh salehti rang mahiyia Awo samaneh awo samaneh kolu di ruskeh naa lang mahiya

Galla goriya teh kala kala thil veh, galla goriya teh kala kala thil veh

Sada kadkeh lehgaiya dil veh

Lateh di chadar uteh salehti rang mahiyia Awo samaneh Awo samaneh kolu di ruskeh naa lang mahiya awo samaneh kolu di ruskeh naa lang mahiya

Galla goriya the kala kala thil veh, galla goriya teh kala kala thil veh

Sanou ajj pichwareh mil veh

Lateh di chadar uteh salehti rang mahiyia Awo samaneh Awo samaneh kolu di ruskeh naa lang mahiya Sanou kan-da tu mariya akh veh, sanou kandah to mariya akh veh

Sadha atteh deh wich haath veh

Lateh di chadar uteh salehti rang mahiyia Awo samaneh Awo samaneh kolu di ruskeh naa lang mahiya

Sadi kandha tu sutiya rasiya sadi kandha tu sutiya rasiya

Tusa puchiya the naa asa dasiya

Lateh di chadar utheh salehti rang mahiyia Awo samaneh

Awo samaneh kolu di ruskeh naa land mahiya

Oh Teri maa neh..oh teri maa neh…

Oh Teri maa neh pakaiya rotiya veh, oh teri maa neh Teri

maa neh pakhiya rotiya

Asa mangiya the pehgaiya souhtiya

Lateh di chadar utheh salehti rang mahiyia Awo samaneh

Awo samaneh kolu di russkeh naa lang mahiya Teri maa neh

banaiyee kheer veh teri maa neh Teri maa neh banaiyee kheer

veh

Asa mangi the peh gai peer veh

Lateh di chadar utheh salehti rang mahiyia Awo samaneh

Awo samaneh kolu di ruskeh naa lang mahiya

Teri maa deh chitteh chitteh dhand veh, teri maa deh chit-

teh chitteh dhand veh

Jedu haasdi teh jee kara phaan veh

Lateh di chadar utheh salehti rang mahiyia Awo samaneh

Awo samaneh kolu di ruskeh naa lang mahiya

Teri maa di lambhi lambhi gutt veh, teri maa di lambhi

gutt veh

Jedu thordhi the jee kara putt veh

Lateh di chadar utheh salehti rang mahiyia Awo samaneh

Awo samaneh kolu di ruskeh naa lang mahiya Lateh di

chadar utheh salehti rang mahiyia Awo samaneh

Awo samaneh kolu di ruskeh naa lang mahiya

Translation (Cotton sheet that has been coloured, come in front of me my Love don't walk past me being upset, the song creates scenarios when she couldn't talk to him so he is sulking and she is trying to bring him round, because he will not accept her gestures she starts to mock his mother.)

Kala shah kala (Geet – song)

Kala shah kala Oh kala shah kala

Merah kala eh sardaar goriya nu daffa karo oh goriya nu

daffa karo

Mein app thileh di taar kala shah kala

Sasariyeh tereh phanj puthar do teen teh do kanastar

Jera mereh haan da oh chalagaiya hai daftar Kala shah kala

Oh kala shah kala

Merah kala eh sardaar goriya nu daffa karo oh goriya nu

daffa karo

Mein app thileh di taar kala shah kala

Sasariyeh tereh phanj puthar do bhangi do sharabi Jera

mereh haan da oh kiriyah phool gulabi

Kala shah kala Oh kala shah kala

Merah kala eh sardaar goriya nu daffa karo oh goriya nu

daffa karo

Mein app thileh di taar kala shah kala

Sasariyeh tereh phanj puthar do devar teh do jhet Jera

mereh haan da oh chala gaiya pardes

Kala shah kala Oh kala shah kala

Merah kala eh sardaar goriya nu daffa karo oh goriya nu

daffa karo

Mein app thileh di taar kala shah kala

Sasariyeh tereh phanj puthar do chooeh do niour Jera

mereh haan da oh betta mereh kol

Kala shah kala Oh kala shah kala

Merah kala eh sardaar goriya nu daffa karo oh goriya nu

daffa karo

Mein app thileh di taar kala shah kala Kala shah kala Oh kala

shah kala

Merah kala eh sardaar goriya nu daffa karo oh goriya nu

daffa karo

Mein app thileh di taar kala shah kala

Translation (My chief has dark skin, push away the lighter

skin people as darker skin people have are perfect in every way, mother inlaw you have 5 sons 4 are bad but my dark skin chief is the best one.)

Boliyan (couplets)

A Boli expresses situations, their emotions and their typical situations. Usually a boli is sung and introduced by one woman, and then the other girls form a chorus.

These boliyan are usually passed down generation by generation orally. This forms a continuous and successive chain, each generation being taught by their predecessor. It is through this process that boliyan have refined and passed on from long ago. Now, boliyan have been fused with Bhangra music

to spread all over the world to North America, Great Britain as well as Australia and New Zealand and mixed with all the cultures it interacts with. This has created a modern, urban style bhangra genre that is listened to by more than just North Indians.

Artists such as RDB have fused the urban style of the United Kingdoms hip-hop music with traditional

Punjabi beats and lyrics which models the new bhangra genre that is described above.

Although women mainly sing boliyan, men also do. His Hit Smash Kulwinder Dhillon, was launched by his song Boli-yan.

"Jaago" the night before the wedding, the awakening night is when all of the family join together and sing boliyan, to celebrate the joyous occasion.

Oreh oreh oreh phaaga waliya deh kaaraj hogai poorer phaagah waliya de kaaraj hogai pooreh

Harrehiya harrehiya khaa bhaag di mallan nu gudheh gud-heh chah

Raya raya raya ajj din kushi ya da phagga deh nal aya ajj din kushiya da bhaga deh nal aya

Bari barsi katana gaiya kat kat ke liyande paaveh Babuleh neh vaar dholiya

Jinu paag banani naah aveh

Bari barsi katana gaiya kat kat ke liyanda patasa… Sohreh kolu kound kadhdi nagha rakhdi calip walla pasa

Bari barsi katana gaiya kat kat ke liyanda sutta Babuleh neh vaar dholiya

Meri kuth deh prandeh nallu chuta

Nukar jandeh ki kat liyondeh, Nukar jandeh ki kat liyondeh

kat kat ke liyondah Anna! Ik meri nath dig pai, nuo

keh chakki jawaana

Nachan wali di adhi na rendhi gouhn waleh da mooh Boli mein pavam,nachleh giddheh wich tu

Bol bol bol veh tu holli holli bol, bol bol bol veh to holli bol

Merah dil tharkeh.

Ajja natch leh gidheh wich meri bhaa farkheh

Ajja natch leh gidheh wich meri bhaa farkheh

Sareh tha gheneh mereh mapehya neh pahai ,sareh tha gheneh mereh mapehya neh pahai

Ikko thaveeth odeh ghar da ni , Jedu lardah teh laadeh laadeh kardah ni

Sareh tha gheneh mereh mapehya neh pahai sareh tha gheneh mereh mapehya neh pahai

Ikko thaveeth odeh bhap da ni

Jedu lardah the bhatereh wangu Chakh da ni

Wagdhi rahee wich udahna pameeriya, wagdhi rahee wich
udahna pameeriya

Bolu veeru penna mangana janjeeriya Bolu veeru penna
mangana janjeeriya

Bolleh bolleh bolleh ajj mreh veereh deh kohn barabar
bolleh ni ajj mereh veereh deh

Cholleh cholleh cholleh ajj mereh veereh deh bhabou
barabar bolleh ni ajj mereh veereh deh

Saas meri neh mundeh jameh

Saas meri neh mundeh jameh, jam jam parri rasoi, sareh

maa vargeh pyou warga na koi

Kadeh hoo karkeh kadeh haa karkeh geerah dedeh ni muti-
yareh lambi bhaah karkeh

Jeh mundiya meri thor tu wekhani jeh mundiya meri thor wekhani garvha leh deh chandi dah

Lakh hileh majajan jandida da

Kadheh na kadeh tereh katteh mitteh jam nu Kadheh na kadeh tereh katteh mitteh jam nu Kadheh the raaj paiya dil mereah

Tumba wajada zalma dil mereh tumba wajada zalma wich mereh

Tar veh tar veh tar veh

Merah udheh doriya melah waleh ghar veh, Merah udheh doriya melah waleh ghar veh

Merah udheh doriya melah waleh ghar veh, Merah udheh doriya melah waleh ghar veh

Merah udheh doriya melah waleh ghar veh, Merah udheh doriya melah wa

Oneh bara kutiya the mein bara rohe oneh bara kutiya the mein bara rohe

Saas sohra soothe naa bachon wala koi

Kat har teh tootiya wellan mein koliya rasoi… Oh raathi

veh raathi Dengar dengar hoi

Veh raati!! Oh raati dengar dengar hoi…

Finally...

I hope you have enjoyed reading this book and I hope that, like me you will want to take part in or at least witness the ladies sangeet. There are many resources available to see some on line and I will be listing links to these and more at the end of the book. If you want to contact me for more information about bookings and/or workshops bet in touch. If you have had experienced the Ladies

Sangeet for yourself and its had an impact on your life I'd love to hear about it and maybe, just maybe I could compile your stories into a book form! Let's keep opening those doors to tradition!

Bibliography

Allami, Abu l-Fazl
Circa 1590Ain-i Akbari. Translated by H. Blockmann.
Delh: 1989. Reprinted by New Taj Office.

Apte, Vasudeo Govind
1987 The Concise Sanskrit English Dictionary. Delhi: Motilal Banarsidas.

Arnold, Alison E.
1991 Hindi Filmi Git: On the History of Commercial
Indian Popular Music Ann Arbor:
University Microfilms International. (Ph. D. Dissertation).

Bagyalekshmy. S.
1991 Lakshanagrandhas in Music. Trivandrum: CBH Publications.

Balagopal, Tara
1982 Learn to Play on Veena. New Delhi: Pankaj
Publications.

Bharatamuni
200 B.C. The Natya Shastra. (Translated by a Board of Scholars), Delhi: Sri Satguru Publications.

Bhatkhande, Vishnu Narayan
1934 A Short History of the Music of Upper India. Bombay, India: reprinted in 1974 by Indian Musicological Society, Baroda.

1993 Hindustani Sangeet - Paddhati (Vol 1 - 4): Kramik Pustak Malika. Hatras:Sangeet Karyalaya.

Bhatt, Vishwambharanath
1962 Sitar Shiksha. Hatras:Sangeet Karyalaya.
Bhattacharya, Dilip
1999 Musical Instruments of Tribal India. New Delhi: Manas Publications.

Bor, Joep
1986-87 The Voice of Sarangi; An Ilustrated History of Bowing in India. Bombay: National Centre for the Performing Arts.

Bose, Narendra Kumar
1960 Melodic Types of Hindustan. Bombay: Jaico Publishing.

Chakravarti, Indrani
1991 "Sarod- Its origin and Evolution". Seminar on Sarod. Calcutta: Sangeet Resarch Academy.

Chakravarty, N.
1982 Vaisnava Sangitsastra. Translated by Gajanana R. Sastri and Madanalal Vyas. Varanasi, India: Shri Gokul Mudranalya.

Chaturvedi. B.K.-
no date - How to Play Tabla. New Delhi: Diamond Pocket Books.

Courtney, David.R
1980 Introduction to Tabla. Hyderabad, India: Anand Power Press.

1985 "Tabla Making in the Deccan". Percussive Notes. Vol 23 No 2: pp 33-34. Urbana: Percussive Arts Society.

1987 "Tata and his Kamakshi Vina". Experimental Musical Instruments. December: pp 5-9. Nicasia, CA :EMI

1988 "The Tabla Puddi". Experimental Musical Instruments. Vol 4 No 4: pp 12-16. Nicasio: EMI.

1989 "An Indian Music Specific Audio Driver". Journal of the Acoustical Society of India. Vol 17 No. 3&4: 269 272. Calcutta: ASI.

1990 "A Low Cost System for the Computerization of North Indian Classical Music" (Doctoral Dissertation) IIAS Greewich University: pp. 200: (available through - University Microfilms International, Ann Arbor: Order Number LD01730).

1991a "The Application of the C=64 to Indian Music: A Review", Syntax , June/July: pp. 8-9: Houston.

1991b Tuning the Tabla: A Psychoacoustic Perspective. Percussive Notes. Vol 29 No 3: pp 59-61. Urbana: Percussive Arts Society.

1992a New Approaches to Tabla Instruction. Percussive Notes. Vol 30 No 4: pp 27-29. Lawton OK: Percussive Arts Society.

1992b "Introduction to Spectrum Analysis" Experimental Musical Instruments. Vol 8, No 1: pp 18-22. Nicasio, CA.

1993 "Mrdangam et Tabla: un Contraste". Percussions: Cahier Bimensiel d' Études et d'Informations sur les Arts de la Percussion. Chailly- en-Biere, France: Vol 28, March/April 1993; pp 11-14.

1993a "An Introduction to Tabla". Modern Drummer. Mt. Morris, IL: October 1993; Vol 17, #10: pp.38-84.

1993b "Repair and Maintenance of Tabla", Percussive Notes, Lawton OK: October 1993; Vol. 31, No 7: pp 29-36.

1994a "The Cadenza in North Indian Tabla". Percussive Notes, Lawton OK: August 1994; Vol.32, No 4: pp 54-64.

1995a "The Cyclic Form in North Indian Tabla", Percussive Notes, Lawton OK: August 1994; Vol.33, No 6: pp 32-45.

1995b Fundamentals of Tabla. Houston TX: Sur Sangeet Services.

2000 Advanced Theory of Tabla. Houston TX: Sur Sangeet Services.

2001 Manufacture and Repair of Tabla. Houston TX: Sur Sangeet Services.

REENA KAUR

2001 Learning the Tabla. Pacific MO: Mel Bay Publications.

2003 Focus on the Kaidas of Tabla. Houston TX: Sur Sangeet Services.

Courtney David R & Chandrakantha Courtney

1995 Elementary North Indian Vocal Houston TX: Sur Sangeet Services.

2003 "Antiquity in Indian Music: Facts Factoids, and Fallacies", Sruti Ranjani: Essays on Indian Classical

Music and Dance: pp 156-171. Sruti: The India Music and Dance Society, USA.

Cousins, Margaret E.

1935 Music of the Orient and the Occident. Madras:

B.C. Paul & Co.

Danielou, Alain

1943 Introduction to the Study of Musical Scales. London: Indian Society.

1954 Northern Indian Music (Vol. 1-2). London: UNESCO.

1968 Ragas of North Indian Music. London: Berrie and Rockliff.

Das, Ram Shankar (Pagaldas)

1967 Tabla Kaumudi (vol. 2). Gwalior, India: Ramchandra Sangeetalaya.

Davies, C. Collin

1949 An Historical Atlas of the Indian Peninsula. Second edition. Delhi: Oxford University Press.

Day, C.R.

1990 The Music and Musical Instruments of Southern India and the Deccan. (first published in 1891). Delhi: Low Price Publications.

Dev, Raja Chatrapati Singh Ju

1964a "Dhrupad-Rag Yaman", Sangeet (Dhrupad / Dhammar Ank) . Hathras , India: Sangeet Karyalaya.Vol. 30.

1964b "Dhrupad-Rag Malkosh", Sangeet (Dhrupad / D h a mmar Ank) . Hathras , India : Sangeet Karyalaya.Vol. 30.

Deva, Chaitanya

1989 Musical Instruments in Sculpture in Karnataka. Shimla: Indian Institute of Advanced Study.

Dutta, Aloke

1984 Tabla, Lessons and Practice. Calcutta: Janabani Printers & Publishers.

Ellingson, Ter

1980 "Ancient Indian Drum Syllables and Bu Ston's Sham Pa Ta Ritual", Ethnomusicology. Vol. 24, No 3. pp 431 452.

Feldman, Jeffrey M. & Alla Rakha

(no date) Learning Tabla with Alla Rakha. Los Angeles: Ravi Shankar Music Circle.

1995 The Tabla Legacy of Taranath Rao. Venice, California. Gigitala.

Ganguly, S.

1981 Introduction to Tabla. Delhi, India: B. R. Printers.

Gangoly, O.C.

1948 Ragas and Raginis. Bombay: Nalanda Publications.

Garg, Lakshminarayan (editor)

1968 Tarana Ank. Hathras, India: SangeetKaryalaya.

1970 Bhakti S angeet Ank. Hathras, India: SangeetKaryalaya.

1984 Hamare Sangeet-Ratna. Hathras, India: Sangeet Press.

1994 Kathak Nritya, A Complete Work on Kathak Dance. Hatras, India: Sangeet Karyalaya.

Ghosh, Nikhil

1968 Fundamentals of Raga and Tala with a New System of Notation. Bombay.

Ghosh, Sharmistha

1988 String Instruments of North India (Vol 1&2). Delhi: Eastern Book Linkers.

Gottlieb, R. S.

1977a The Major Traditions of North Indian Tabla Drumming. Munchen, Germany: Musikverlag Emil Katzbichler.

1977b The Major Traditions of North Indian Tabla Drumming. Transcriptions :Munchen, Germany: Musikverlag Emil Katzbichler.

Grant, Michael

1971 Atlas of Ancient History. America: Dorset Press.

Grierson, Sir Abraham

1903 Linguistic Survey of India

Ibrahim, Adil Shah

1956 Kitab-i-Nauras. (ed by Nazir Ahmad). New Delhi: Bharatiya Kala Kendra.

Jairazbhoy, N.A.

1971 The Rags of North Indian Music: Their Structure and Evolution. Middletown CT: Wesleyan University Press.

Jha, Narayan

1983 "Tal Prabhand: Panch Talon Men Yaman- Kalyan", Sangeet (Tal Ank). Hathras, India: Sangeet Karyalaya. Vol. 14: Edited by Prabhulal Garg.

Jingasu, Chiranjiv Lal

1964a "Dhrupad-Rag Hindol", Sangeet (Dhrupad / DhammarAnk) . Hathras , India : Sangeet Karyalaya. Vol. 30.

1964b "Dhrupad-Rag Miyanmalhar", Sangeet (Dhrupad / Dhammar Ank). Hathras, India: Sangeet Karyalaya.Vol. 30.

Kapoor, R.K.

no date Kamal's Advanced Illustrated Oxford Dictionary of Hindi- English. Delhi, India: Verma Book Depot.

Kaufmann, Walter.

1968 Ragas of North India. Calcutta: Oxford IBH Publications.

Kippen, James

1988 The Tabla of Lucknow. Cambridge, Great Britain: Cambridge University Press.

Kothari, K.S.

1968 Indian Folk Musical Instruments. New Delhi: Sangeet Natak Akademi.

Krishnaswamy, S.

1965 Musical Instruments of India. Delhi: Publications Division, Govt. of India.

Leake, Jerry

1993 Indian Influence (Tabla Perspective), Series

A.I.M. Percussion Text (Second Edition). Boston: Rhombus Publishing.

Lele, V.

1983 Sathsangat. Puna, India: V. Joshi and Co.

Mallory, J. P.

1989 In Search of the Indo-Europeans; Language Archaeology and Myth. London: Thames and Hudson Ltd.

Misra, Bhagirat

1984 Kabir Bani. Indore: Kamal Prakashan.

Mital, Prabhudayal

1960 Sangeet Samrat: Tansen: Jivani aur Rachanaen. Mathura, India: Sahitya Samsthan.

Mrdangacharya, B. D.

1976 Mrdang-Tabla -Prabhakar (vol. 1). Hathras, India: Sangeet Karyalaya.

Mrdangacharya, Bhagavan Das and Ram Shankar Das (Pagaldas)

1977 Mrdang-Tabla -Prabhakar (vol. 2). Hathras, India: Sangeet Karyalaya.

Mukherji, D.P.

1975 Indian Music - An Introduction. Bombay: Kutab Publications.

Nathani, Sultan

1992 Urdu for Pleasure: For Gazal Lovers. Bombay: Sultan Nathani.

Neuman, Daniel M.

1980 The Life of Music in North India. Detroit: Wayne State University Press.

Nevile, Pran

1996 Nautch Girls of India: Dancers, Singers, Playmates. New York, Paris, New Delhi: Ravi Kumar Publisher.

Omchery, Leela and Deepti Omchery Bhalla (editors)

1990 Studies in Indian Music and Allied Arts (Vol 1-5). New

Delhi: Sundeep Prakashan.

Oxford University Press

1986 The Oxford School Atlas. New Delhi: Oxford University Press.

Pathak, R.C.

1976 Bhargava's Standard Illustrated Dictionary of the Hindi Language. Varanasi: Bhargava Bhushan Press.

Patnakar, R. G.

1977 Tal Sopan.(vol. 2) Bulandshahar, India: Sangeet Kala Kendra.

1978 Tal Sopan.(vol. 1) Bulandshahar, India: Sangeet Kala Kendra.

Perera. E.S.

1994 The Origin and Development of Dhrupad and it Beearing on Instrumental Music. Calcutta: K. P. Bagchi and Company.

Popley, H.A.

1950 Music of India. Calcutta: YMCA Publishing House.

Prajnananda, S.

1960 Historical Development of Indian Music. Calcutta: K.L. Mukhopadhya.

1963 History of Indian Music (vol. 1). Calcutta: Ramakrishna Vedanta Matha.

1965 Historical Study of Indian Music. Calcutta: Anandadhara Prakashan.

Ranade, G.H.

1939 Hindusthani Music. Poona: Aryabhushan Press.

Ranade,G.S.

1971 Hindustani Music and Outlines of its Physics and Aesthetics. Bombay: Popular Prakashan.

Randel, Don Michael

1978 Harvard Concise Dictionary of Music. Cambridge: Belknap Press (Harvard University Press).

Rangacharya, Adya

1966 Introduction to Bharata's Natya-Sastra. Bombay, India: Popular Prakashan.

Rao, B. Subba

1980 RAGANIDHI- A Comparative Study of Hindustani and Karnatak Ragas: Volume 1. Madras, India: The Music Academy.

1982 RAGANIDHI- A Comparative Study of Hindustani and Karnatak Ragas: Volume 2. Madras, India: The Music Academy.

1984 RAGANIDHI- A Comparative Study of Hindustani and Karnatak Ragas: Volume 3. Madras, India: The Music Academy.

1985 RAGANIDHI- A Comparative Study of Hindustani and Karnatak Ragas: Volume 4. Madras, India: The Music Academy.

Rosenthal, Ethel

1973 Story of Indian Music and its Instruments. New Delhi: Oriental Book.

Sambamoorthy, P.

1960 History of Indian Music. Madras: Indian Music Publishing House.

1962 Catalogue of Musical Instruments Exhibited in the Govt. Museum. Madras: Govt. of Madras.

Sangeet Natak Akademi

1968 Who's Who of Indian Musicians. New Delhi: Sangeet Natak Akademi.

"Sanheetika"

1971 Sitar Visheshak. Allahabad: Sangeet Sadan Prakashan.

Sankaran, Trichy

1994 The Rhythmic Principles & Practice of South Indian Drumming. Toronto: Lalith Publishers.

Shankar, Ravi

1968 Ravi Shankar: My Music, My Life. New Delhi, India: Vikas Publishing House Pvt. Ltd.

Sharangdev

1978 Sangeet Ratnakar. Translated by R.K Shringy and P rem Lata S harma. Varanasi: Motilal Banarasidas.

Sharma, Bhagavat Sharan

1973 Tal Prakash. Hathras, India: Sangeet Karyalaya. 1977

Tal Shastra. Alighar, India: B. A. Electric Press.

Shepherd, F. A.

1976 Tabla and the Benares Gharana. Ann Arbor: University Microfilms International. (Ph. D. Dissertation).

Shrivastava, Girish Chandra

1978 Tal Parichay (vol. 2). Alahabad, India: Sangeet Press.

1979 Tal Parichay (vol. 1). Alahabad, India: Sangeet Press.

Shrivastava, H. C.

1973 Kathak Nrtya Parichay. Alahabad, India: Sangeet Press.

Singh, Anandram "Tomar"

1978 Tabla ke Kuchh Aprachalit Bol, Tal Ank. Hathras, India: Sangeet Karyalaya.

Stewart, R. M.

1974 The Tabla in Perspective. Ann Arbor: University Microfilms International. (Ph.D. Dissertation).

Strangways, A. H. Fox

1965 Music of Hindostan. Oxford: Clarendon Press.

Subbarao, I.V.

1962 Studies in IndianMusic. Bombay: Asia Publishing House.

Tagore, Rabindranath

1961 Ravindranth Thakur ke Sau Geeton ka Swarlipi. New Delhi: Sangeet Natak Akademi.

Tagore, S. M.

1896 Universal History of Music. Calcutta.

1965 Hindoo Music. Varanasi: Chowkhamba Sanskrit Series.

Vashisth, Satya Narayan

1977 Tal Martand. Hathras, India: Sangeet Karyalaya.

1981 Kaida aur Peshkar. Hathras, India: Sangeet Karyalaya.

1982 Aprachalit Kaiyade aur gaten. Hathras, India: Sangeet Karyalaya.

Vyas, Ramkrishna

1977 Rag Pravin. Allahabad, India: Sanjiv Art Press.

Willard, Captain N.A.

1934 A Treaties on Music of Hindustan. Calcutta 1934

Acknowledgements

I owe some of my knowledge to the existence of Wikipedia and the Internet for its vast source of material. Without which I would not have been able to write this book.

www.ladiessangeetbyreenakaur.co.uk

Printed in Great Britain
by Amazon